IMAGES OF WAR

U-Boats at War
in
World Wars I and II

RARE PHOTOGRAPHS FROM WARTIME ARCHIVES

JON SUTHERLAND AND
DIANE CANWELL

Pen & Sword
MARITIME

First published in Great Britain in 2009 by
PEN & SWORD MARITIME
an imprint of
Pen & Sword Books Ltd,
47 Church Street,
Barnsley,
South Yorkshire.
S70 2AS

A CIP record for this book is available from the British Library.

ISBN 978 1 84884 0454

Typeset by S L Menzies-Earl

Printed and bound by CPI UK

Pen & Sword Books Ltd incorporates the Imprints of
Pen & Sword Aviation, Pen & Sword Maritime, Pen & Sword Military,
Wharncliffe Local History, Pen & Sword Select, Pen & Sword Military
Classics, Leo Cooper, Remember When, Seaforth Publishing and
Frontline Publishing.

For a complete list of Pen & Sword titles please contact
Pen & Sword Books Limited
47 Church Street, Barnsley, South Yorkshire, S70 2AS, England
E-mail: enquiries@pen-and-sword.co.uk
Website: www.pen-and-sword.co.uk

Contents

Imperial-Metric Unit Conversion

1 inch (in.) = 0.0254 metre (m)
1 foot (ft) = 0.3048 metre
1 yard (yd) = 0.9144 metre
1 mile = 1.6093 kilometre (km)
1 ton (t) = 0.907 tonne (te)

Introduction

The submarine, or as the Germans would refer to it, *Unterseeboot* (*U-Boot*), and hence the anglicised U-boat, was originally designed, of course, as a vessel for underwater exploration. The original design is believed to have been created in 1620 by Cornelius Drebbel, a Dutchman working for King James I. One hundred and fifty years later it had been transformed into a weapon of warfare. *Turtle* was used during the American War of Independence. Submarines were also used during the American Civil War, but it was at the end of the nineteenth century that the submarine came of age in terms of development. Diesel-electric propulsion and the periscope all made the submarine, or U-boat, a viable tool of war.

At around the beginning of the twentieth century, tests were under way using internal combustion engines for surface movement, and electrical battery power for work undersea. Large numbers of submarines were ready to be deployed when the First World War broke out in August 1914. As in the Second World War, in terms of personnel involved and vessels deployed, submarines had a disproportionate impact both in real and in psychological terms. Both naval and merchant shipping were in grave danger, and both the British and the Germans in particular, in each war, used these vessels in an attempt to starve one another of food and resources.

Enormous steps forward were made between the wars. The submarine, equipped with a small seaplane, became a vital reconnaissance unit ahead of a surface fleet. Although the Germans had a limited surface fleet in line with the restrictions of the Treaty of Versailles, they had the largest submarine fleet. They confidently expected to beat the Royal Navy through undersea warfare.

As in the First World War, the hunting grounds were the Atlantic, the North Sea and even more remote locations. In the Second World War the Germans created 'wolf packs' that literally hunted and destroyed whole convoys and their escorts. Until 1943 they had unprecedented success, but sonar and radar advances, along with the breaking of German naval codes and the ability to detect their radio transmissions, were to lead to enormous German losses. This would pave the way for the amphibious attacks on enemy-occupied Africa and Europe in Operations Torch, Husky and Overlord.

While the British tended to use their submarines in a blockading role, the Germans, as we will see in both wars, used them as an offensive arm, hunting and destroying armed and civilian vessels alike, and often vessels of neutral powers. A contributory factor to the USA entering the First World War in 1917 was the sinking of RMS *Lusitania*. Although it was a British vessel, and in later years was also believed to have been a blockade runner carrying munitions, its destruction off the coast of Ireland by *U-20* was universally condemned as a war crime, and helped galvanise US public support behind President Woodrow Wilson.

For the first time a unique collection of photographs from the First World War of U-boats in action, belonging to Friedrick Pohl, a warrant officer who served on *U-25* and *U-33*, is now being featured, along with photographs taken by the highly successful U-boat commander, Otto Wünsche. Wünsche commanded four different U-boats between 1914 and November 1918 (*U-25, U-70, U-97* and *U-126*).

There are also two collections of unique Second World War photographs, the first from the collection of Günther Prien, who commanded U-47 until he and his crew were lost in March 1941. The second collection formerly belonged to Herbert Brüninghaus. Although he commanded three different U-boats between 1941 and 1943, Brüninghaus did not undertake any combat patrols. However, his collection of photographs provides a fascinating account of life in the German *Kriegsmarine* during a period where the German navy was the least prepared for the war in 1939, yet achieved remarkable results against overwhelming odds.

We are indebted to the owner of these albums, James Payne, for his permission to use them in this photographic record of German U-boat warfare and *Kriegsmarine* life across two world wars.[1] They were wars in which the men operating in these vessels often served for weeks or months without a break in near-impossible conditions, constantly hunted and in the certain knowledge that if they were discovered and were unable to surface and surrender then death was inevitable. In the First World War alone, of the approximately 360 German U-boats that had been constructed over half had been lost, but they managed to account for over eleven million tons of shipping sunk.

As in the First World War, German U-boat crews proved that eighty or so men could do far more damage at a fraction of the cost than over a thousand men on a battleship during the Second World War. Although they had limited underwater speed, endurance and range, they were significantly better underwater performers than their First World War counterparts. Their contribution was enormous to the German war effort; they were led by Admiral Karl Dönitz, who himself had been a U-boat captain in the First World War. Indeed so successful were his tactics that U-boats presented an even graver threat to Britain and her ability to continue to resist and ultimately strike back than the *Luftwaffe*.

Throughout the Second World War, at a cost of around 800 U-boats, a staggering 80% of all of those in operation, or two-thirds of the total production, had sunk

14.5 million tons of shipping. Or to put a more personal face on it, they had ter-rorised 3,000 crews by destroying their ships.

The German surface fleet during the Second World War was comparatively far weaker than it had been in the First World War. It neither attempted, nor was it given the opportunity, to challenge the dominance of the Royal Navy. It would have been a very short and bloody engagement that the Germans could not possibly have won. But by switching to submarine warfare, the Germans could range far and wide across the Atlantic, into the northern seas and slip into the Mediterranean and beyond, hunting for prey and turning them from the hunted to the hunter. These photographs tell part of these remarkable men's story – the dark raiders, the stealthy predators of the sea, who rarely gave and rarely received mercy.

---

1 Any reader wishing to obtain a set of high-resolution scans of these photographs can do so through James Payne at www.throughtheireyes.org.uk

Chapter One

The *Kriegsmarine*

The German *Kriegsmarine*, or navy, was reformed in May 1935 after the German government had passed the Law for the Reconstruction of the National Defence Forces. At the end of the First World War Germany had only been allowed to retain a small defensive military force and a tiny defensive navy, the *Reichsmarine*. The *Kriegsmarine* itself consisted of three main components – naval vessels, naval formations and ground-based units. There were thousands of ships and many hundreds of naval formations and ground units. During the period 1939–45, over 1.5 million served in the *Kriegsmarine*; around 65,000 were killed, 21,000 wounded and 105,000 posted missing.

At times both the army (*Heer*) and the air force (*Luftwaffe*) fought with overwhelming numbers against an enemy. But the *Kriegsmarine* never had this advantage except in a handful of operations and theatres for short periods of time. It fought on almost every front but suffered from a lack of effective co-ordination. The bulk of the vessels with any offensive capability were destroyed by the Allied air forces or naval powers. But the smaller vessels of the *Kriegsmarine*, and indeed many of the submarines, continued to operate until the unconditional surrender documents were signed in May 1945. The smaller vessels were responsible for thousands of miles of coast, and this was not the sole contribution of the *Kriegsmarine*.

Ground units manned the Atlantic Wall in the west, and many manned flak and artillery units. Others served as infantry, engineers and communication units. Some were still fighting on the ground during the battle for Berlin.

The *Kriegsmarine* was disbanded by the Allied Control Commission in August 1946. Our focus, however, is on the U-boat crews and their officers. Training programmes for the men had been introduced in 1927, although without U-boats much of it had been theoretical. Some of the men had served on Turkish vessels, which provided invaluable insights. In May 1932 it was decided that training for prospective submariners would be intensified. It would now last for twelve weeks, with 207 hours of teaching and up to two hours a day on a simulator. The first course took place at Kiel in the summer of 1933, and the second in September 1934. There were lectures on maintenance, torpedo handling and firing, the use of the periscope, understanding the power units and machinery, and practical models were built of the periscopes, gyrocompasses and steering equipment. Practical training took place on a simulator fitted into a minesweeper.

As training continued and Type IIB U-boats became available for training purposes, even more refinements were brought into the training exercises. Crews would have to carry out sixty-six surfaced and sixty-six submerged practice attacks before they could fire their first live torpedo. They would have to perform many of the manoeuvres at night. The desire was to improve their seamanship, understand the sea and the wind and, above all, refine their tactics.

Dönitz, driving the direction of the training and organisation, believed he knew what was necessary. Routines were vital, as was tactical training, and they practised zigzagging, silent operations, diving and surfacing techniques, surface gunnery and anti-aircraft defence. In the period from 1936 to 1939 the U-boat fleet doubled in size. The training continued to be intensive. The commander courses had begun at the beginning of 1933, first with theoretical training and then again by using the simulators.

Once the first U-boats had been launched, enough men were passing through the training schools to provide crews for around sixteen submarines. The training boats themselves were immediately pressed into active service in September 1939, but after the Polish campaign many of them became available once more (with the exception of the Norwegian campaign in 1940). The training programme had to be enormously expanded. The schools were now to produce fifty-four crews (1940), 250 crews (1941) and 350 crews (1942).

In 1940 the training was transferred from Neustadt to Pillau. Training allowed for ten days' sea time for crew members and up to eighteen days for officers and non-commissioned officers. The key component for officer training was underwater manoeuvres, although some non-commissioned officers were also shown how to use hydroplanes and diving manoeuvres.

The most important officer on the submarine was the commander. Many of them had joined the U-boat force as early as 1936. Many of them had been naval officers in other fields. Early in the war a commander had to be at least 25 years old, but later the limit was lifted. Ludwig-Ferdinand von Friedeburg became the youngest U-boat commander on 15 August 1944, having celebrated his 20th birthday just three months earlier. Usually the limit in terms of age was 40 years. During the course of the war some 1,410 commanders served, and around 574 of them died during the war. The ranks for commanders can appear to be somewhat confusing, but the most common rank was either *Oberleutnant* or *Kapitän-leutnant* (two former U-boat commanders had reached the rank of *Admiral* by the end of the war).

The U-boat crew itself consisted of a chief engineer, an executive officer, a chief quartermaster, a warrant officer machinist, a chief boatswain's mate, and a number of ordinary seamen, technical seamen, control-room crew, radio personnel, torpedomen, gunnery crew and a cook. There would also be a doctor, perhaps a war correspondent, a meteorologist, an intelligence officer and anti-aircraft crewmen.

The basic requirement for a naval recruit was that they were between 17 and 23 years of age. Parental consent was required for those under the age of 21. The navy was particularly interested in acquiring men with a skilled trade, such as a mechanic or an electrician. Naval crews would sign on initially for a four-year minimum period, which did not include a year as a trainee. A naval recruit could volunteer for any branch of the service.

Unlike British crewmen, German *Kriegsmarine* personnel from 1938 onwards had a universal ribbon around their caps, which simply said *Kriegsmarine*, rather than identifying the name of the ship. The sailor's cap itself was usually relegated to formal occasions, and a boarding cap, which was essentially a dark blue, wool side-cap, was generally worn. Typically the men would wear wide-leg trousers and a pullover shirt in dark blue. This was a uniform worn up to the rank of petty officer. Generally the uniform would be white in good weather and dark blue in winter. In cold weather a dark blue, double-breasted jacket would be worn over the shirt, and for parades a short, waist-length jacket, commonly known as a monkey-jacket, was worn.

Warrant officers wore straight-leg trousers, white shirts with black ties and double-breasted reefer jackets. They wore peaked service caps with either a dark blue or a white top. Officers were recognisable owing to the number of sleeve rings, and their peaked caps showed their rank grouping by the amount of embroidery.

In working conditions many of the men wore their white clothing, which, although it was white, was extremely hardwearing and easy to wash. The navy also issued a hardwearing denim working-jacket, which was primarily an olive or green/brown colour.

The following collection of photographs features U-boat crew members primarily in non-combat situations, and presents a further valuable insight into the lives of German *Kriegsmarine* officers and men.

A shot of a German Type VII submarine coming into dock, with the crew parading on deck. Note the launches running alongside with photographers taking shots. In 1935 the German navy was renamed the *Kriegsmarine*. Between the wars it had been known as the *Reichsmarine*, and in the First World War the *Kaiserliche Marine*. After 1938 the Germans abandoned any pretence that they were following the requirements of the Treaty of Versailles, which limited the size of their navy. Plan Z was finalised in 1938, which called for the building of a navy of around 800 vessels in the period 1939–47. The predominant vessel would be the submarine, of which the Germans planned 249.

A close-up of the same German submarine, focusing on the conning tower. Note how this has developed compared to the earlier First World War vessels. It is far more prominent, and provides a better observation post. It also offers far more protection to the crew member. The Germans still only had around 78,000 men in the navy when war broke out in September 1939.

Quickly the expectations of a land victory after the ignominious fall of France in 1940 led to Plan Z being shelved. The primary focus would now be on the construction of U-boats. This is *U-47* commanded by Günther Prien. She was commissioned on 17 December 1938 and was lost on 7 March 1941.

A close-up of the bow of a German submarine, lashed along a quayside. Even by wartime standards, life aboard a U-boat was harsh. War patrols could last anything between three weeks and six months. Crews relished the opportunity to enjoy time on dry land. While at sea they could not shave or take a bath, and they rarely managed to change their clothes.

A number of German vessels in port, including the Type VII submarine. The U-boat was essentially a watertight steel cylinder with a pressure hull. Outside the pressure hull was a thinner, aerodynamic hull that effectively streamlined the boat when it was submerged. Steering was achieved by rudders and hydroplanes, but when the U-boat was submerged it was virtually blind. The U-boat operated just like many other vessels, with propellers and rudders, but it would have to be in motion in order to turn. The U-boat could adjust its buoyancy by using its ballast tanks. To submerge, the ballast tanks were flooded with water, and to surface, compressed air was blown into the ballast tanks.

A *Kriegsmarine* U-boat officer. Typical U-boat crews were organised into officers, chief petty officers and seamen. This individual is either an officer or a chief petty officer. A boatswain, for example, would be responsible for crew discipline, although other petty officers were specialists dealing with the torpedoes, steering or the engines.

A torpedo being fired from a German surface vessel. A number of different torpedoes were used during the Second World War. Broadly, they were either steam or electrically powered. Their main purpose, of course, was to destroy enemy ships. The submarine crews referred to them as eels. Torpedoes made it possible for submarines to attack while they were still submerged. They were very sophisticated and extremely expensive. They consisted of the pistol, warhead, depth-keeping device, propulsion and guidance system.

Kriegsmarine crew at a training facility. Ordinary crew members were known as seamen, or *Matrosen*. They acted as a watch crew on deck, manned guns, and loaded torpedoes or were cooks. Many of the crew members were specialists; some were machine men, radio men or torpedomen, but they would be expected to work on a variety of tasks. The crews would normally work three eight-hour shifts. They would sleep one shift; carry out regular duties in another and miscellaneous tasks on the third.

These *Kriegsmarine* seamen pose for a group photograph at a function. They all have *Kriegsmarine* NCO trade badges on the left arm of their uniforms. A U-boat war badge in bronze was introduced by *Grossadmiral* Erich Raeder in October 1939. It was awarded to all ranks of U-boat personnel who had served on two war patrols or had been wounded in action.

U-boat officers. The commanding officer of a U-boat would be a *Kapitän-leutnant* or an *Oberleutnant zur See*. His second-in-command would be the first watch officer. This executive officer would shadow the commanding officer and be prepared to take command should the need arise. Beneath them was the second watch officer, who was responsible for the watch crew, the flak gun and deck gun, as well as the radio room. The final officer was the leading engineer, responsible for the engines, motors and batteries.

Two U-boat ordinary seamen. Note that the seaman on the left of the picture carries his cap in such a way that we can see *Kriegsmarine* rather than the name of his vessel. The men are wearing their *ausgehanzug* uniform. This was a blue service-suit for walking out, consisting of a jacket, a pair of trousers, a white and a blue shirt. The shirt collar had three stripes. They were also issued with a silk neckerchief, grey gloves and a cap. Rank badges were on the left sleeve. It appears that these two men are *Matrosen*, or ordinary seamen.

These men are wearing their characteristic bell-bottomed white service-trousers and also have on their white service tops. They are also wearing their *Schiffchen*, or forage caps. These was worn by many *Kriegsmarine* ranks. Traditionally the crewmen would wear their blue shirts and caps between October and April, and the white ones for the remainder of the year. During the war years blue caps tended to be worn at all times.

This is an unidentified German U-boat in shallow waters, either under construction or being repaired. Owing to Germany's geographic position, obviously all of the shipyards and repair yards prior to the outbreak of the Second World War were on the north coast, bordering either the North Sea or the Baltic. Most were concentrated around the Kiel and Hamburg areas. Some nineteen yards in eleven locations built 1,153 U-boats that were commissioned during the period 1935–45. This was in addition to yards that concentrated mainly on midget submarines.

Another unidentified German U-boat under way, but passing a point in the harbour. The Germans created sixteen combat flotillas during the Second World War, only one of which remained stationed in Germany itself, at Kiel (5th Flotilla). All of the other flotillas at various times were located in facilities as far afield as Salamis in the Mediterranean, St Nazaire and Brest in France, and Narvik and Trondheim in Scandinavia.

Kriegsmarine seamen in their ordinary field dress. Towards the end of the war increasing numbers of *Kriegsmarine* personnel were allocated to ground combat roles, and would effectively operate as ordinary infantry or artillery. With the exception of the insignia there would be very little difference between these men and regular army soldiers.

This is a fascinating mixture of uniforms and caps, as worn by German U-boat officers and petty officers. The two men with the white jackets are wearing a version of the Collani designer jacket, and both have their blue forage caps. The other two men are wearing more formal service wear. The officer on the far right, according to his cap badge, is an *Oberleutnant* or *Kapitän-leutnant*.

Kriegsmarine seamen in a posed shot, seen manning the anti-aircraft gun. At the beginning of the war the standard U-boat anti-aircraft armament was the 20 mm flak gun. It was some distance from the conning tower, and the problem was that the conning tower itself provided a dead zone in terms of firing at incoming aircraft. The flak gun also had to be removed and stowed before diving. Subsequently the weapon was relocated and given a special platform close to the conning tower. By 1942 twin or quadruple 20 mm guns were being used on the U-boats, although most of these were not introduced until the middle of 1943. At the end of the year the 37 mm gun was introduced. This final version was specially adapted, and could fire fifty rounds per minute. It had an effective range of 16,800 yards.

This photograph shows *Kriegsmarine* seamen in predominantly white uniform, with an array of small-arms, including rifles and a machine-pistol. Even U-boat crewmen would be trained to use small-arms so that they would be effective as boarding parties and able to defend themselves onshore. Note the ammunition pouches attached to the waist belts, and that some of the crewmen have shoulder-straps attached to their belts. A tripod-mounted machine-gun is clearly visible in the centre of the picture.

This is a posed shot of a U-boat crew on dry land, in their standard work wear. On war patrols fresh water was limited to drinking water only, as in many cases one of the water tanks would be filled with diesel fuel to extend the operational range of the submarine. Washing and showering were not allowed. The men were only allowed to have with them the clothes that they were wearing, as locker space was at a premium. They only had one tiny locker for their personal belongings. Some of the men would live and sleep in the forward torpedo room, which was used as crew quarters to maximise the limited space. At the beginning of a war patrol, six of the bunks had to be folded up to allow room for a pair of additional torpedoes. Only when these had been fired off would each man have his own bunk. Washing was normally carried out using a salt-water sponge-bath, and a form of Cologne was used, known as Kolibri, in order to control body odour.

A full *Kriegsmarine* crew complement, or class, shown in this photograph on parade at a training facility, presumably in Germany. Once the men were on board their submarines literally months could pass before they set foot on land once again. By the end of their war patrols many of the men would emerge with full beards, and filthy uniforms and bodies. Even going to the toilet was not straightforward; initially only one toilet was available, as the second one was used as a food storage cupboard. Forty to fifty men would be sharing the same toilet, which had a hand-pump. The contents were hand-pumped into the sea. It was prohibited to use the toilet when enemy vessels were close by.

A crewman carrying out washing duties on board a submarine. Note the pile of plates and cutlery to his left. Food was crammed into every nook and cranny on the U-boats. There were only small refrigerators on board, which meant that fresh food quickly spoiled in the damp atmosphere. Loaves of bread quickly sprouted white fungi, which the crews nicknamed rabbits because they were white and fuzzy. The crew often referred to the soya-based filler issued to U-boat crews, *Bratlingspulver*, as diesel food, as it quickly took on the taste and aroma of diesel.

Chapter Two

The U-Boats of World War One

Germany was one of the last of the major powers to begin a submarine-building programme for her navy. In many respects she followed the British model, developing and experimenting with new submarine designs rather than putting them into full production and then discovering that there were operational or constructional problems. While the British intended to use the submarine to defend bases and the coastline, the German navy's intention was to use them as an offensive arm.

The key battle area would be the North Sea. This meant that any submarine deployed by the Germans would have to have a good operational range, the ability to remain at sea in the challenging winter months and a good surface speed, along with a high level of reliability.

It was not until February 1905 that the German navy awarded the first contract to build a submarine to the Germania Yard at Kiel. *U-1* would be a 238-ton vessel with a kerosene engine and a single 45 cm bow torpedo-tube. One of the problems was that the kerosene created clouds of white smoke that could be seen for miles. Nevertheless, *U-1* was finished in December 1906, and in the meantime a second and larger submarine had been commissioned to be built at the Imperial Dockyard at Danzig – *U-2*. In August 1907 two more slightly larger submarines, *U-3* and *U-4*, were also ordered. It transpired that *U-1* was unable to meet the operational requirements of the German navy, and the engine was not reliable enough.

The German navy was looking for a vessel that had a 2,000-nautical-mile surface endurance, a speed of 10.5 knots underwater, a surface speed of 15 knots, four torpedo tubes, two bow tubes and the ability to supply a crew of twenty with seventy-two hours' air supply. Although the next twelve submarines were built with these specifications in mind, they did not fulfil them.

By 1912 it was still considered to be practicable only for the submarines to be out operationally for five days, working no more than 300 nautical miles from their base. In effect this meant they could operate on the eastern side of England and just into the English Channel from Heligoland.

The German's first submarine casualty took place on 9 August 1914, when *U-15* was rammed and sunk by HMS *Birmingham*. *U-13* had been due to return from patrol on 12 August, but she failed to appear, in all probability having struck a German mine.

The German submarines had more success the following month when on the morning of 22 September *U-9* sank three British cruisers, HMS *Aboukir*, HMS *Cressy* and HMS *Hogue*. She also managed to sink the cruiser HMS *Hawk* on 15 October.

Technically, the U-19 Class of German submarine was an enormous step forward. It had a diesel engine, 50 cm torpedo tubes; it was much larger and longer and it also had six torpedo tubes. This type of vessel would provide the blueprint for many of the German submarines up to *U-116*.

Later on in the war larger submarines were ordered by the German navy, but many of these vessels were never completed. Those that were completed were often named after early German submarine heroes. *U-140*, for example, was named after *Kapitän-leutnant* Weddigen, who had commanded *U-9* in 1914 but had been killed in action in *U-29*.

The Germans also deployed mercantile submarines, notably *Deutschland* (*U-155*). She was a blockade runner carrying cargo to and from the United States. She made two trips in 1916. *Bremen* accompanied her on the second trip but never arrived. A third, *Oldenburg*, was converted into a cruiser U-boat before she was completed. Ultimately *Deutschland* was also converted, with a pair of bow torpedo tubes and a pair of 15 cm guns.

Later in the war an improved version of this submarine cruiser was proposed, with six torpedo tubes and heavier guns. *UD-1* was started but never completed.

When the Germans overran parts of Belgium in 1914 they acquired Bruges and Zeebrugge, both of which would be ideal submarine bases and, of course, closer to the proposed areas of operation. The Germans decided to introduce smaller coastal submarines. These were ordered in November 1914 and came into service at the beginning of 1915. They were known as Type UB submarines, just 88 ft 7 in. long, with a displacement of 127 tons and a pair of torpedo tubes. The idea was that they would be built in sections, transported by rail and then assembled at their base. The first was *UB-1*, which would operate in the Adriatic. The Type UB-3 came into service during the 1917–18 period. It was much larger: 182 ft long, a displacement of 520 tons and five torpedo tubes. These were such a success that they were to prove to be the blueprint upon which the Germans would design their Type VII U-boats for World War Two.

The Type UB submarines were designed for coastal operations. A smaller, Type UC, of which there were two variants, was also designed as minelayers. These too were transported by rail for final assembly, but the early ones had no means of offence or defence, although later models had torpedo tubes.

The British captured *UC-5* and made a careful examination of the wreck of *UC-2*. This helped them enormously in unravelling German mining strategy and allowed the British to modify their own E Class submarines as minelayers.

There were also smaller Type UE ocean-going minelayers that had torpedo tubes. The later submarines in this series could operate off the United States coastline. A further Type UF coastal submarine was also planned. This was similar to *UB-2* but would have four or five 50 cm torpedo tubes, but the Germans did not manage to complete any of these before the end of the war.

At the beginning of World War One the Germans had around twenty operational U-boats working with the High Seas Fleet. Initially they were deployed as a defensive screen; however, within days an ambitious plan was hatched to launch an attack on the British Grand Fleet at Scapa Flow. This was the operation in which *U-15* was lost. *U-5* and *U-9* turned back because of engine problems, and *U-18*, although it managed to penetrate Scapa Flow, was sighted and sunk on 23 November 1914. Overall the German U-boats had lost 20% of their strength without claiming a single kill.

September 1914 had been a more promising month: *U-21*, commanded by Otto Hersing, had sunk the British light cruiser, HMS *Pathfinder*. He was to become a U-boat ace, launching twenty-one war patrols over a three-year period in which he sank thirty-six ships, including two battleships. As we have already seen, *U-19* had claimed the three British destroyers off the Hook of Holland in September.

On 20 October 1914 an event took place that was to set the scene or terms of engagement for both world wars. Off southern Norway *U-17* engaged the British steamer, SS *Glitra*. *Kapitän-leutnant* Feldkirchner boarded the vessel to inspect the cargo, after which he allowed the crew to board lifeboats, and then he sank the steamer.

On 26 October the pattern continued when *Kapitän-leutnant* Schneider on *U-24* torpedoed SS *Admiral Ganteaume* without warning in the Dover Strait. This was the first time that a merchant vessel had ever been attacked in this way. Henceforth merchant vessels would become the prime target in attempts to wreck the economy of a wartime foe.

The significance of these two events was not lost on either the British or the Germans. The British had already mounted a blockade of Germany at a distance. Now the Germans felt confident enough to be able to launch their own counter-blockade. Had they been able to maintain this blockade throughout the war perhaps the Allied victory would have been compromised.

By the end of 1914 the Germans had lost five U-boats, but had sunk ten merchant vessels and eight warships. On 18 February 1915, unrestricted U-boat warfare was introduced by the Germans. Henceforth any vessel found around the British Isles would be sunk without warning. Deciding whether a vessel was truly neutral was at the discretion of the U-boat captain.

The Germans lost Weddigen in March 1915 when *U-29* was rammed by the British battleship HMS *Dreadnought*. His vessel was lost with all hands.

One of the most notorious submarine incidents took place on 7 May 1915. *Kapitän-leutnant* Schwieger, commanding *U-29*, fired a torpedo at RMS *Lusitania* to the south of Ireland. She sank in eighteen minutes and 1,200 people lost their lives, including 128 Americans. Controversy still rages around the loss of the vessel. She was registered as part of the British Fleet Reserve, she was in a war zone and arguably she was carrying munitions. However, such was the storm of protest from neutral America at the loss of her civilians that the German submarines were now ordered to ignore passenger liners.

On 19 August 1915, there was a similar but less well-known incident. *Kapitän-leutnant* Schneider (*U-24*), believing RMS *Arabic* to be a troop transport, sank her. But among the forty-four dead were three Americans. The Germans feared a backlash from the Americans, and as a consequence, on 20 September 1915, the U-boats were withdrawn from British waters, and for a while the primary area of operations became the Mediterranean.

By the end of 1915 the Germans had lost twenty U-boats, but had claimed 855,000 tons of shipping. The UC minelayers had claimed another ninety-four vessels. However, on 24 March 1916, *UB-29*, commanded by *Oberleutnant* Pustkuchen, sank the French cross-channel ferry, *The Sussex*, which had been mistaken for a minelayer. Eighty people were killed, among them twenty-five Americans. There was another enormous diplomatic row, and this time the Germans withdrew all of their vessels on 24 April.

For the Allies the losses were beginning to be serious, and new counter-measures were needed. Up to this point, with depth charges still under development, a submarine could only be destroyed by ramming it or hitting it while it was on the surface. The British now created the Q-ship.

As far as the U-boat was concerned, the Q-ship would look like a tramp steamer, but in reality it was armed with guns and torpedoes, and its cargo was wood or cork, in order to make it almost unsinkable. The Germans discovered to their cost that these Q-ships were incredibly dangerous. *U-36* was sunk by HMS *Prince Charles* on 24 July 1915. Less than a month later *U-29* was sunk by HMS *Baralong*. One of the hardest-fought engagements between a Q-ship and a U-boat took place on 8 August 1917, when an eight-hour battle took place between *UC-71* and HMS *Dunraven*. In all, Q-ships managed to destroy fourteen U-boats and damage sixty others. Twenty-seven Q ships were lost.

In October 1916 U-boats returned to British waters, and in that month alone they sank 337,000 tons, and between November 1916 and January 1917 another 961,000 tons. In February 1917 a further 520,000 tons were sunk. U-boat successes steadily continued, reaching a peak in April 1917, when 860,000 tons were sunk.

With the USA finally declaring war on Germany in April 1917, the numbers of potential merchant victims soared. In the period May 1917 to November 1919, 1,134 convoys, consisting of 16,693 merchant vessels, made their way back and forth across the Atlantic. This new convoy system would lead directly to the defeat of Germany: she simply could not stop the flood of munitions, supplies and men. The tide had certainly begun to turn against the German U-boat threat.

According to the Armistice the 176 operational German submarines were handed over between November 1918 and April 1919. The German navy had started the war with twenty-eight U-boats; 344 had been commissioned and 226 were under construction when the war ended. The Germans had sunk over twelve million tons of shipping, or 5,000 ships. Seven submarine commanders, headed by Lothar von Arnauld de la Perière (450,000 tons) topped the list. The U-boats had been seen to be a powerful, though not a decisive, weapon of war. The 176 operational U-boats handed over to the British were evaluated, stripped, parcelled out to Allies or scrapped. Germany was then prohibited from building or possessing U-boats.

This is *U-23*, which was launched in April 1912 and commissioned in September 1913. She had a relatively short career, stretching from 1 August 1914 to 20 July 1915, during which time she launched three patrols. She managed to sink seven enemy vessels. Her four commanders were Erwin Weisbach, Hans Adam, Egewolf Freiherr von Berckheim and Hans Schulthess. The final commander led the crew between January and July 1915. On 20 July *U-23* was torpedoed by the British submarine *C27* working in conjunction with the decoy trawler, *Princess Louise*. Twenty-four of *U-23*'s crew were killed, and there were just ten survivors. *U-23*'s short career claimed five British vessels: *Invergyle* (13 March), *Fingal* (15 March), *Chrysolite* (19 May), *Crimond* (19 May) and *Lucerne* (19 May), a Danish vessel, *Martha,* (15 May) and a Norwegian vessel, being the largest at 3,735 tons, *Minerva* (22 May). Initially *U-23* was assigned to the IV Flotilla, although it was later assigned to the III Flotilla.

These are *U-23* and *U-25*, probably in Kiel harbour during the first year of the war. *U-25* was ordered in March 1911, launched in July 1913 and commissioned on 9 May 1914. Her commander during her most productive period (1 August 1914 to 15 September 1915) was Otto Wünsche. Wünsche's first kill was the Norwegian ship *Glittertind* on 7 June 1915. This was to be the first of seven Norwegian vessels that Wünsche's crew would claim, along with a Russian ship (*Anna*, 8 July 1915), a Swedish vessel (*Maj*, 6 August 1915) and no fewer than thirteen British vessels. Many of the victims of *U-25* were relatively small, most being under or around 200 tons. The largest victim was the British vessel *Guido*, at just under 2,100 tons, on 8 July 1915. Ultimately, *U-25* would survive the war. She was surrendered to the French on 23 February 1919 and broken up at Cherbourg between 1921 and 1922.

A close-up of the crew, including Wünsche, preparing the vessel before departing on a war patrol. Note the deck gun and the loading of supplies from a launch. Wünsche was born in Duisburg on 28 September 1884. It appears that he joined the German navy in 1903 and had become a *Leutnant* by September 1905. By 1908 he had become an *Oberleutnant*. In November 1913 he had risen to the rank of *Kapitän-leutnant*. Wünsche would be awarded both the first-class and the second-class Iron Cross, the Hausorden von Hohenzollern (May 1917) and the Pour le Mérite (20 December 1917). He would not only command *U-25* between August 1914 and September 1915, but go on to command three other submarines during his wartime career. From September 1915 until October 1917 he commanded *U-70*, then *U-97* until January 1918. His final command, *U-126*, was for just one month until the war ended in November 1919. It was during his command of *U-97* that he received his award in December 1917. While in command of the first three vessels he sank a total of 182,000 tons of enemy shipping: collectively seventy-six ships sunk, including one warship, and six further vessels damaged. Otto Wünsche died in Kiel on 29 March 1919.

A view of the crew of *U-25* at sea. Note the sleeping crewman beside the deck gun. The aircraft marked 412 is probably a Friedrichshafen FF33. The company, Friedrichshafen Flugzeugbau, was founded in 1912 and located at Lake Bodensee, which was famous for its association with the Zeppelin airship industry. Ultimately the company would take over many of the production facilities, but in turn the company itself would be bought by Dornier. Friedrichshafen Flugzeugbau was well known for its construction of seaplanes for German naval aviation. The FF33 was a single-engine amphibious reconnaissance biplane, originally designed in 1914. The main production model was powered by a Benz inline engine. It had longer twin floats than the two initial versions, and consequently this pictured variant is almost certainly the FF33E, of which 180 were built. It has a radio transmitter instead of an armament. Many different versions of this aircraft were built and used by not only the Germans, but also the Bulgarians, Danes, Finns, Dutch, Poles and Swedes.

U-25 was a Type Mittel U submarine, and four of these were commissioned, *U-23* to *U-26*. All of them were constructed in Kiel. They had a surface displacement of 685 tons and a submerged displacement of 878 tons. Their top surface speed was 16.4 knots and a submerged speed of 9.7 knots. Their range on the surface was 8,790 miles at 8 knots and a submerged range of 80 miles at 5 knots. They carried six torpedoes and had two bow and two stern tubes. The deck gun, which can be clearly seen in the photograph, was a 105 mm piece for which the submarine carried 300 rounds. There was a crew of thirty-five and the craft was able to operate to a maximum depth of around 160 feet.

The deck gun on *U-25* was an ideal defensive or offensive weapon against smaller boats and ships, particularly when use of the torpedo was limited. The deck gun was often used to conserve torpedoes. German submarines would often use them to finish off merchant ships or to engage vessels that had straggled behind a convoy. Usually three men operated the deck gun – a gunner, a layer and a loader. Shells, each weighing around 23.3 kg, were brought up from a watertight locker. Note that the gun does not have a shield, as this would impede the progress of the submarine under water. Theoretically the range was around 16,400 yards, although sitting targets would be engaged at a closer range. The U-boat actually made a very poor gun platform, and it would rarely be used against armed enemy vessels, as the submarine would be seriously outgunned.

Albis Norge, a Norwegian steamer of 1,381 tons, was built by Nylands Verksted in Christiania in 1896. *Albis* had the misfortune to encounter Otto Wünsche's *U-25* on 14 August 1915 when she was some sixty miles west-north-west of Stat, in Norway. She was carrying a cargo of pit props and was making her way from Archangelsk to Immingham, the sister port of Grimsby in north-east Yorkshire. Immingham was actually a British submarine base during the First World War. *U-25* sank *Albis* using the deck gun, having ordered the crew to abandon ship. There were no casualties when *Albis* went down.

Five days after the sinking of *Albis Norge*, *U-25* intercepted *Bras Norge*, another Norwegian steamer, of 1,863 tons. She had been built in West Hartlepool by W. Gray & Co. Ltd in 1889. She was being operated by Bras of Skien, unlike *Albis*, which was being operated by Camilo Eitzen & Co. Wünsche sank her after capturing the ship off Egersund. *Bras Norge* was also carrying pit props and was *en route* from Göteborg to Blyth in Northumberland. *U-25*, having evacuated the crew, sank *Bras* using the deck gun, and there were no casualties.

An action shot of *U-25*'s deck gun in the process of sinking *Bras Norge* on 19 August 1915. The conditions seem perfect for gunnery practice against the helpless Norwegian steamer. Note the shell casings on the deck of the submarine and the fact that many of the crew members have come on deck in order to witness the sinking of the merchantman. In recognition of Wünsche's contribution during the First World War, not only was he awarded several gallantry medals, but in May 1940 the vessel *Otto Wünsche* was launched, being commissioned in November 1943 at Kiel. She was a submarine tender, and after the war she was taken by the Russians and renamed *Pechora*. She sank in the Barents Sea, near the Norwegian border, in the 1970s.

This unidentified steamer, marked *SH 192*, was also sunk by Wünsche in *U-25* in 1915. It is probable that the vessel was a British merchantman, which narrows down the identification to *Nottingham*, *Pentland*, *Saturn* or *Velocity*, all of which were smaller vessels sunk on 7 June 1915. Alternatively, the ship could be *Cardiff*, *Castor*, *James Leyman* or *Tunisian*, all of which were sunk on 9 June. Wünsche also sank *Sunbeam* on 4 July 1915, and *Hainton*, *The Syrian* and *Fleetwood* on 11 July, but it is unlikely that this vessel is *Guido*, as this was over 2,000 tons and was sunk on 8 July 1915. This photograph clearly shows the vessel seconds before it sank.

These are the dying seconds of the French steamer *Antonie*, a 2,698-ton French vessel built in 1910 by Atel and Chant de France of Dunkerque. It was being operated by Cie des Chargeurs Français (Plisson et Cie) of Bayonne. The loss of *Antonie* is actually credited to *U-33* on 3 October 1915. She was sunk in the Cerigo Strait, which is between the Peloponnese and the Greek island of Crete. *U-33* had been operating in the Aegean to great effect, and together with *U-39* had managed to sink eighteen steamers. Just the day before the sinking of *Antonie* the two submarines had attacked *Arabian*, a British merchant ship, in virtually the same position. *U-33* was at the time commanded by Konrad Gansser. Gansser commanded *U-33* between 27 September 1914 and 23 September 1916. Prior to this he had operated for a month on *U-8*, and after his stint on *U-33* he commanded *U-156* until June 1918. During the war Gansser's crews claimed forty-nine ships, with a total tonnage of 142,538 tons.

A view of the Norwegian mail and passenger steamer *Iris Norge*, in June 1915. In an article published by the *New York Times* on 16 June the Norwegians, as a neutral country, were making strenuous protestations against German submarine attacks on neutral merchant ships. Even at this early stage of the war, Norway had lost more than any other country. They described the attacks as being made by 'treacherous German submarines'. *Iris* operated as a mail and passenger steamer between Newcastle and Bergen. This may be a photograph of one of the two attacks that she suffered. On one occasion she was hit by a torpedo but did not explode, and on the second occasion the torpedo missed her by a matter of inches. Although this photograph was in the collection of Friedrich Pohl, who served as a warrant officer on *U-25* and *U-33*, it is unclear which of these two vessels launched the attacks.

Kapitän-leutnant Otto Wünsche, on the deck of *U-25* in the summer months of 1915. Wünsche is shown in the centre of the photograph, and is clearly in a relaxed mood with two of his fellow officers. Wünsche would go on to command *U-70*, in which he would sink the British sloop *Rhododendron* and fifty-three civilian ships. Among the civilian ships was *Southland*, which was a Belgian ocean liner that had been built as the SS *Vaderland* in 1900. It was being used during the First World War to transport officers and men of the Canadian Expeditionary Force from Halifax to Liverpool. *Southland* had previously been fortunate, as she had already been torpedoed in September 1915 by *U-14*. After undergoing repairs she was sunk by Wünsche's *U-70* in June 1917. She went down 140 miles north-west of Tory Island, off the Irish coast, with the loss of forty-four lives.

Kapitän-leutnant Otto Wünsche; this time seen standing by the deck gun of *U-25*, also during the summer months of 1915. It is unclear as to precisely which port this is, but it is most likely to be the port of Kiel. Of the four *U-23* Type Mittel submarines, *U-23* itself was lost on 20 July 1915, and *U-26* on 30 September 1915. This vessel was lost in the Gulf of Finland, and although the actual reason for its loss is unknown, it is clear that all thirty crew members were killed during the incident. *U-24* was surrendered on 22 November 1918 and broken up at Swansea. The most successful of this type, *U-25*, was surrendered to the French on 23 February 1919 and broken up at Cherbourg over the winter months of 1921/2.

This is *Nordaas Bergen*, which was sunk by Otto Wünsche's *U-25* on 9 July 1915. She was intercepted while carrying a cargo of coal from Blyth to Petschora in the Barents Sea in northern Russia. The vessel was 1,111 tons, a Norwegian steamer built in 1914 by Mossvaerft and operated by Fr. Walter of Bergen. The steamer was intercepted some thirty miles east of Aberdeen. Again it appears that *Kapitän-leutnant* Wünsche's men engaged the hapless Norwegian steamer with the deck gun.

The period from June to August 1915 saw a particularly productive period for *U-25*. *Nordaas Norge* was the second Norwegian vessel that Wünsche's crew managed to sink, and until that point was the third largest vessel that they had sunk. The Norwegians would lose another five vessels in August 1915 to *U-25*, two of which were even larger than *Nordaas Norge*.

The dying moments of *Nordaas Norge*, as she is brought under sustained fire from the 105 mm deck gun on board *U-25*. It was not always intended that the Type Mittel U submarines would have a single 105 mm gun. Originally some had been fitted with 88 mm guns, while others had both. By 1917 all of the vessels that broadly followed the Type Mittel U, of which there were forty-six, were refitted with the 105 mm gun.

Norman Norge on fire. The shot is taken from the deck of *U-25* on 7 August 1915. *Norman Norge* had been built in Windsor, Nova Scotia, Canada, in 1869 and, as can be seen in the photograph, was a sailing vessel. She was 1,060 tons and operated by A. Bestbye of Fredriksvaern and Larvik. This Norwegian vessel was carrying a cargo of pit props and was *en route* from Nesoya, which is a small island in the municipality of Asker in Norway. The area is now effectively a suburb of Oslo. The area is most well known for being the place where *Maud*, the ship that was sailed by Roald Amundsen through the North-East Passage, had been built. Subsequently she served as a supply vessel for the Hudson Bay Company.

A second photograph of *Norman Norge* taken from the deck of *U-25*. Note the clear Norwegian markings on the side of the ship in a vain attempt to prevent attacks on this neutral vessel. Wünsche's crew intercepted her around eighteen miles off Arendal, a port on the southern coast of Norway. Arendal had a long maritime tradition and was originally established in the 1500s. The sinking of *Norman Norge* would have been in sight of the Store Torungen lighthouse. It had been constructed in 1844 and only electrified a year before *Norman Norge* was sunk. The lighthouse remains in use. *Norman Norge*'s crew was evacuated from the vessel before *U-26* sank her, presumably with the deck gun.

This is a photograph of *Arendina*, a small Dutch sailing vessel. This photograph was taken by the crew of *U-25*. There is no reason to believe that she is under attack. There is no record of this *Arendina*, and it should not be mistaken for the *Arendina* that lies off the coast of north County Donegal, at Redcastle. This vessel sank in 1852, carrying wheat from the Danube and bound for Derry. There is another *Arendina* that was stranded at Gaso, Lysekll, Sweden, on a voyage from Harlingen to Moss with a cargo of roof bricks. She had been built in 1838 at Veendam. She sank in just over forty feet of water in September 1855.

This is a shot of *UB-3*, a UB-1-type coastal torpedo-attack boat. The vessel was ordered in November 1914 and commissioned in March 1915. She was commanded by Siegfried Schmidt between 24 March and 23 May 1915. She scored no successes in terms of sinking enemy vessels, and she was lost in the Aegean Sea, but the cause of her loss was unknown. All fourteen crew members were killed when she was lost.

A shot from *U-25* as she pulls alongside a German navy surface vessel in rough seas. If a German submarine still retained the bulk of its ammunition and torpedoes, it could be resupplied at sea with food and other provisions, rather than returning to base. Alternatively, the surface vessel could be escorting the submarine into base. Note that ahead of the two vessels is what appears to be a tug, although neither the submarine nor the German naval vessel appears to be under tow.

Members of the crew of *U-25* coming alongside in a small rowing-boat. Note the open hatch that houses the rowing-boat. Also note that the deck gun has been taken down and stowed below. Routine checking of the superstructure of the submarine would be necessary whenever possible, as even minimal damage could cause catastrophic damage if she were submerged. Normally this procedure would only take place if the submarine crew was sure that it was not under threat from detection by enemy aircraft or surface vessels.

A larger rowing-boat alongside *U-25*. Note that the officers appear to be handling maps or plans and that the deck gun has been brought up. The two men in the rowing-boat appear to be civilians, and this may suggest that they are members of the crew of a merchantman, and that the nautical maps from the merchantman have been taken by the submarine for intelligence purposes.

Another shot from the quayside, probably at Kiel, of *U-25* undergoing maintenance and repairs. Routine maintenance was absolutely essential between war patrols, particularly at this early point in submarine warfare. The vessel and its crew would be helpless if there were a mechanical failure while on a mission, as they would find it incredibly difficult to return to base.

U-25 making headway in a heavy swell. Note that the deck gun is deployed and ready for action. Whenever possible the German submarines would remain on the surface, constantly scanning the skies and the horizon for enemy aircraft and vessels.

Another shot of U-25 under way. The vessel appears to have just surfaced, and this photograph has been taken from the conning tower.

Another photograph taken from the conning tower seconds later. The crew is beginning to come on deck. The sky is overcast, and this may well mean that the submarine is safe from aerial observation and can now make better progress on the surface.

Several of the crew are on deck in their dark blue work uniforms. The submarine is flying recognition flags, and the German naval flag is also visible. In all probability the vessel is either coming into or leaving port. Note the large ship in the distance under steam to the right of the photograph, and the marker buoy to the left.

Otto Wünsche and two of his senior officers on board *U-25*, in the conning tower, wearing their oiled waterproofs. Note that the waterproof hats are designed to go over the peaked caps that they appear to be wearing.

An action shot of *U-25*'s deck gun in action. Three crewmen are manning the gun itself on its pivoting base, while a fourth man brings up additional ammunition from the stowage locker. By the angle of the gun the crewmen appear to be trying to hole an enemy vessel close to the water line. A hit breaching the hull at this point would send the victim down in a matter of minutes.

Officers of *U-25* consult their maps and work out their bearings. Note that the officer in the centre is presumably the duty watch officer, as he has his binoculars around his neck. He is also wearing winter clothing.

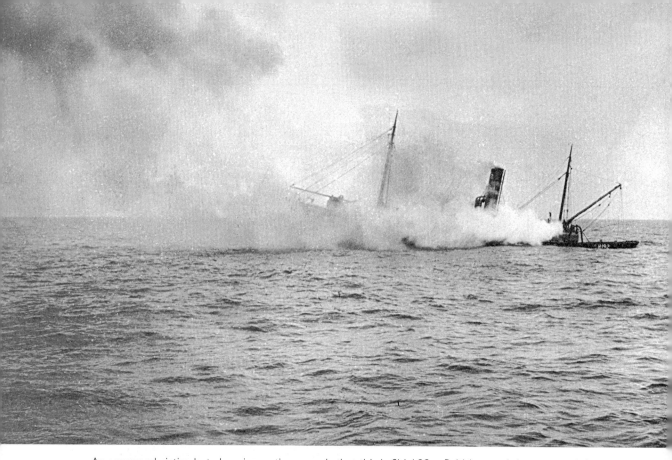

An unnamed victim, but close inspection reveals that this is *SH 192*, a British vessel that was sunk by *U-25* in the summer of 1915. The prodigious amount of smoke has been caused by seawater rushing into the engine room and beginning to extinguish the coal-burning engines.

The very last seconds of *SH 192* as she sinks beneath the waves, stern first. The number can be clearly seen on the bow.

Another victim of *U-25*. This again may be *SH 192*, but taken from a different angle. Her stern is almost completely submerged and it is possible to see the underside of her keel as she tips backwards to her watery grave.

A dramatic photograph taken from *U-25* of the last seconds before a merchant victim sinks for ever beneath the waves. This is a remarkable photograph, given the shutter speed of the camera and the rapid progress of the sinking of this vessel. The attack appears to have been made in relatively calm conditions.

This sailing-ship is presumably another of the smaller victims of *U-25* in the summer of 1915. The submarine may have just surfaced close to her, as it is possible to see some crewmen still on board. Although it is impossible to identify this ship precisely, it is likely to have been one of the smaller vessels that *U-25* sank in June, July or August of 1915. In all likelihood she is a British ship of under 200 tons.

Another unnamed ship encountered by *U-25* in the summer of 1915. It is not possible to identify her, even though her name is tantalisingly out of focus on her stern and she clearly carries a flag. There appears to be peculiar lifting-gear on her bow, which may suggest that she is not a simple cargo vessel.

A close-up of the hatch on the conning tower of *U-25*. A crewman is already on watch. He wears his white uniform trousers and a tight-fitting short jacket as protection against the elements. Note that the hatch is secured by a simple rope.

This is another unidentified but Norwegian vessel encountered by *U-25* during the summer months of 1915. We can clearly see from the flag that she is a Norwegian ship, and written on her hull is partially visible '*Nor*'. Her name is obscured by the crew in a lifeboat. Clearly *U-25* has ordered them to evacuate the ship prior to their vessel being sunk by the deck gun. Speculatively this may be *Norman Norge*.

Another shot of a Norwegian victim of *U-25*. Once again she is flying the Norwegian flag on her stern and there are Norwegian stripes on her hull. A rowing-boat is pulling alongside, but there are still several crew members near the stern of the vessel. Again, unfortunately, it is not possible to identify her.

Crewmen from a merchantman who have evacuated their vessel on instruction from *U-25*. If it was possible, the submarine would take the evacuees on board rather than casting them adrift in open water. Many of the attacks were made, however, close to the coastline, so it was possible, after several hours of exhausting rowing, for the crew to safely pitch up ashore. By that time, of course, their vessel would be sunk and the submarine would be many miles away.

Crew of a merchantman in a rowing-boat alongside *U-25*. They appear to have either just cast off or are passing close to the submarine, as there is no attempt on board the submarine to secure the rowing-boat. These men are lucky, as in the First World War it was more likely for submarines to demand evacuation prior to sinking the vessel, rather than make unexpected attacks that would sink the ship with all hands.

U-25's own small rowing-boat. A package is being thrown from or to it. This could either be booty that has been taken off a merchantman or even mail for the crew from a supply ship.

U-25 approaching base in choppy water. Unfortunately it is not possible to identify the coastline, but note the two lighthouses; one to the extreme right and the other amid the buildings in the centre of the photograph. The photograph appears to have been taken from beside the conning tower of *U-25*.

A shot of another victim of *U-25*. She is listing heavily to the right, and the submarine is establishing a distance from her before she goes down. The submarine would ideally remain in position until the crew were assured that the victim was finished, but they would have to keep their distance.

Chapter Three

The U-Boats of World War Two

Under the terms of the Treaty of Versailles, Germany had been forbidden to retain or build any submarines. In actual fact the greater part of her fleet that was to take to the seas in 1939 was barely four years old. In the period 1919–34 German submarine development had continued. Her vessels had been built in foreign shipyards to German design, and co-ordinated and controlled by German technicians. Vessels were built in Turkey and in Finland, for example.

Gür was built in 1932 for the Turkish navy. She was 237 ft 6 in. long with a submerged displacement of 960 tons, and had six torpedo tubes and one 102 mm gun. *Vesikko* was built in Finland in 1933, and was essentially a coastal submarine, 133 ft 10 in. long with three torpedoes, a small gun and a submerged displacement of 300 tons. *Vesikko* was essentially the prototype of the Type II U-boat, and *U-1* was launched in Kiel in June 1935. Further refinements were made until the Type IID was brought in in 1940, a larger vessel with a longer range. The Type I was based on *Gür*, as well as *UB-49* from the First World War. These would become known as the Type VII, and they would become the mainstay of the German submarine fleet.

U-27, designed to be used in the Atlantic, was launched in 1936. *U-30* was a Type VIIA, and she sank the liner *Athena* at the beginning of the war. The first Type VIIB was launched in April 1938; it had better engines and could carry more fuel. *U-47*, a Type VIIB, was commanded by *Korvettenkapitän* Günther Prien. He managed to penetrate Scapa Flow in 1939 and sink HMS *Royal Oak*. He was to go on to have a very successful war in the Atlantic.

The Type VIIC was brought in in 1940; it could carry more torpedoes, was more able to defend itself against aircraft attack and had a longer range. The German navy placed an order for 688 of them.

By the time Germany surrendered in 1945, 705 submarines of the Type VII had been brought into service. Of this total, 437 had been lost in action. Remarkably, *U-977* in 1945 was based in Norway, and rather than surrender, it made a sixty-six-day submerged passage to Argentina, arriving there on 17 August 1945. The crew were interned.

This was by no means the largest German type of U-boat. The Type IX had a far greater range. The first, *U-37*, came into service in August 1938. There were gradual refinements, giving these submarines an even greater range.

As the Germans had attempted to do in World War One, submarines were also used to carry cargo. The Type IXC had a cargo-carrying capacity of 252 tons, and was perfectly capable of travelling from Germany to the Far East. Type XB submarines were built as ocean-going minelayers with a range of 14,000 nautical miles. In order to increase the patrol endurance of their Type VII submarines, the Germans also developed a Type XIV, essentially a fuel tanker. It could carry 203 tons of fuel and four torpedoes that could be transferred to the Type VIIs.

Germany was desperately trying to create what she perceived to be a true submarine: in other words a vessel that did not have to spend a great deal of time on the surface, but could travel at a good speed under water. This became imperative as the Allies wrestled air superiority from the Germans in almost every theatre of war.

The key development was the *Schnorkel*, or snorkel. This allowed the submarine to be ventilated, enabling the submarine to use her diesel engines while she dived. In effect it was a long tube with a float-valve. The valve closed when it went below the water. Another development was the invention of the *V-80* with a turbine engine. It broke down a high concentration of hydrogen peroxide to create oxygen and steam. Hydrogen peroxide, however, was very volatile. The Germans tested the *V-80*, which was a small submarine, and planned to apply it to the Type VII, but it never got further than the planning stage.

Other developments were the Type VIIA (1943). These too relied on the turbine engine, but also had standard diesel-electric drives. The Germans continued to experiment, desperately trying to create a submarine that could quickly dive and stay beneath the water for a considerable period of time and maintain a good underwater speed.

The Type XXI was a brand-new development of the design. It was streamlined and had high-capacity batteries. It would be capable of maintaining an underwater speed of 18 knots for ninety minutes; it would carry twenty-three torpedoes and have six bow tubes. It would also have impressive anti-aircraft and anti-ship armament. However, it would be useless for operations in the North Sea and English Channel because of its size.

Further variants were designed in 1944. The other major development was the XXIII, which used many of the developments of the XXI but was intended for coastal use. It would only have two torpedo tubes, and was considerably smaller, with a fraction of the displacement of the monster XXI. By August 1944 the Germans were giving priority to the construction of the XXI and the XXIII over the VII, but by this stage Allied bombing was making fabrication increasingly difficult. Between mid-February and mid-April 1945 no fewer than fourteen Type XXIs, which were virtually ready to become operational, were destroyed by Allied aircraft while still in Bremen, Hamburg and Kiel.

The first and only Type XXI to become operational was *U-2511*, and even then she was only launched on 18 March 1945. She left for her first operational patrol on 30 April out of Norway, but on 4 May, before she had even fired a single torpedo, she was ordered to surrender.

U-2321, the first Type XXIII, was launched from Hamburg in April 1944. Two further Type XXIIIs (*U-2324* and *U-2322*) were launched between the end of January and the beginning of February 1945. In all, five Type XXIIIs carried out eight operational patrols.

On 17 August 1940 the Germans declared a total blockade of the British Isles. This was despite the fact that the German navy wanted a far more modest declaration to be made. It was in no way ready to enforce such a rigid total exclusion zone. But Germany was determined not only to sweep the British from the skies, but also to starve them as a prelude to invasion. The German navy would be expected to play its part in this.

As far as the German navy was concerned, the war had broken out five years too early; it was simply not ready. It had insufficient surface vessels and did not yet have a truly reliable and sufficiently large submarine force. The development of the submarine force had been the responsibility of Karl Dönitz. The primary target for the submarines was not enemy warships but their merchantmen. In order to beat Britain, her overseas trade needed to be interdicted, and food, munitions and vital supplies sent to the bottom of the ocean. Dönitz was of the opinion that a handful of submarines had no hope of achieving this, and he believed and wrote in a memorandum dated 1 September 1939 that he would need 300 submarines: 100 in the operational area, 100 *en route* or on their way back and 100 undergoing refitting and training in dock. As it was, he had fifty-seven, and only twenty-seven of them were capable of operating in the Atlantic.

Despite this, there was a very early success, as we have seen, when Prien penetrated Scapa Flow. This was not to be the last catastrophic loss at the hands of German submarines. Dönitz was firmly of the opinion that the Type VIIC (1942) was undoubtedly the best submarine in the world, but in reality it was relatively antiquated. Improvements were made by adding snorkels, anti-aircraft batteries, better torpedoes and shortwave transmitters. Germany desperately needed a new generation of submarines, but this was becoming increasingly difficult as systematically each and every German submarine shipyard was pulverised from the air. In the first two years of the war German submarine losses were relatively low, but this was not to be the experience of the majority of the submariners. In 1940, for example, the Germans were winning the loss-to-launch ratio: fifty-four were launched and twenty-six were lost. Dönitz needed, in order to keep up the pressure, forty new submarines a month. At best Germany was managing no more than twenty.

The most critical phase of the submarine programme was in 1942. The German navy wanted far more men and resources to be thrown into the U-boat campaign. During the year 238 submarines were brought into service, but eighty-eight were lost. By the peak of the battle of the Atlantic in 1943, German submarine wolf packs were inflicting grievous losses on the Allies. It appeared for a time that Germany was winning the war in the Atlantic. Then things began to change.

Convoys were zigzagging away from U-boat patrols as if they knew precisely where they were located. The submarines, when they picked up radio signals that had always led them to their prey, now found that the merchantmen were nowhere to be seen. The Germans could not discover the answer to the riddle, although every scrap of information was scrutinised. Had the wavelengths of the submarines been compromised? Or were enemy aircraft using unknown wavelengths? Before they could reach any conclusions, in May 1943 the Germans lost thirty-five submarines and managed to sink only 96,000 tons. Dönitz called off the Battle of the Atlantic, telling Hitler: 'Our losses are too heavy. It is now essential that we conserve our strength, since otherwise we would merely play into the enemy's hands.'

He went on to say, on 2 June: 'Under the present circumstances, it is pointless to send the U-boats out to fight. If there are enough shelters, it would be best to keep them there in safety until they can be equipped with new weapons.'

This was to mark a sea change in deference to the growing resources and power of the Allies. Henceforth, Dönitz believed that the submarines had to be used offensively still; otherwise they would be forced to fight a defensive war that they could never win. Hence the rationale behind the submarine warfare until the end of the war and the reason why thousands more German submariners would be doomed to die. The German submarines had not been betrayed except by themselves. The Allies were now picking up their radio signals and using radar that was effectively making the submarines helpless. They could now track the U-boats that were themselves shadowing convoys. But there was worse – the German codes had been cracked.

The Allies had outmanoeuvred the German submarine force, but it continued to fight on. There was no other real option for the Germans, though the last time

German surface vessels ventured into the Bay of Biscay was December 1943. They found themselves hounded by the Royal Navy. The surface vessels were now reduced to coastal operations, yet the U-boats still roamed the Atlantic. Having failed to prevent men, munitions and supplies from reaching Britain, and unable to penetrate to any great extent the intricate network of Allied vessels, aircraft and minefields protecting the Allied entry point into mainland Europe, the submarines could not hope to make a major strategic impact on the course of the war.

By the time Germany finally accepted unconditional surrender in May 1945, only 150 submarines were left, little more than 15% of her vast, 1,000-strong submarine fleet. They hoisted black flags, and the Royal Navy led them to their destruction. Operation Deadlight saw them scuttled *en masse*.

A host of Type II coastal boats. Most of these were designed for use as training-boats after they had been deployed for brief periods of time in 1939 and 1940. These early submarine types, which were commissioned in the mid-1930s, were primarily used as school boats. *U-2*, for example, suffered two attacks in April 1940, once by the British submarine HMS *Unity* in the North Sea, and on a second occasion, five days later on 10 April, by a Wellington that attacked it with bombs to the south-west of Norway. *U-2* sank on 8 April 1944 after it collided with a German steam trawler, *Helmi Söhle*. Seventeen of *U-2*'s crew were killed.

This is a close-up of *U-1*, which was launched in June 1935. During its short career it had three commanders – *Kapitän zur See* Klaus Ewerth, *Kapitän-leutnant* Alexander Gelhaar and *Korvettenkapitän* Jurgen Deecke. Ewerth was killed on 8 November 1943 in the central Atlantic aboard *U-850*. Gelhaar died in the north Atlantic on 14 October 1939 when *U-45* was sunk. Deecke was killed on 6 April 1940 when *U-1* was sunk. It is believed that *U-1* hit a British mine in Barrage Field No. 7. All twenty-four of the crewmen were killed. The mines had been laid on 3 March. An alternative explanation is that *U-1* hit a mine laid by the British submarine HMS *Narwhal*.

This is another view of *U-1*. Deecke had become an officer in the German navy in April 1931. This was his first U-boat command, having taken over *U-1* on 29 October 1938. *U-1* only managed two patrols, a total of eighteen days. She had left Wilhelmshaven on 15 March 1940 and returned safely without incident on 29 March. On 4 April she left her base once more but was sunk two days later. This Type II saw four different variants, marked A to D. They were highly manoeuvrable, had a rapid dive time and were very durable. Early on in the war they were withdrawn from service and assigned to full-time training. They had been built in contravention of the Treaty of Versailles. However, public construction was not announced until the signing of the Anglo-German Naval Agreement in February 1935. Type IIs were small, and they were often described as dugout canoes owing to the fact that they rolled so much in heavy seas.

This is the Type II submarine *U-6*. She was launched in August 1935 and commissioned in September of the same year. She was to have a long and eventful career, primarily as a school, or front, boat. Throughout her career she would have a number of commanding officers, the most important of whom, as far as this collection of photographs is concerned, was Herbert Brüninghaus. *Kapitän-leutnant* Brüninghaus commanded *U-6* on two occasions, between October 1941 and August 1942, and once again between September 1942 and October 1942. Although Brüninghaus did not undertake any wartime patrols, he was to go on to command *U-148* between October 1942 and January 1943, and *U-1059* between May 1943 and September 1943. *U-148* was another school boat, but *U-1059*, a Type VIIF, under the command of *Oberleutnant* Günter Leupold, who took over from Brüninghaus, was sunk to the south-west of the Cape Verde Islands by depth charges dropped by Avenger and Wildcat aircraft belonging to USS *Block Island*, an American escort carrier. She was sunk on 19 March 1944. Forty-seven of the crew were killed and there were just eight survivors. It is not clear whether Günter Leupold survived the attack.

An unidentified Type II submarine is shown in this photograph. It did not have a deck gun and only carried five torpedoes. It had a maximum speed of 13 knots on the surface and 6.9 knots when submerged. Normally it would have a crew of between twenty-two and twenty-four men.

This Type VII is probably in Kiel, and is preparing to leave port along with several other German navy surface vessels. The Type VII was considered to be a new generation of attack U-boats. They were more powerful than the Type IIs. There were a number of variants, but the Type VIIC was considered to be the workhorse, and 568 of these vessels were commissioned between 1938 and 1944. It was a slightly modified version of the successful VIIB, of which twenty-four had been constructed. The Type VIICs were primarily built in Kiel, Danzig and Hamburg, although others were built in Emden, Rostock, Lübeck, Stettin, Wilhelmshaven, Flensburg and Bremen. The Type VIIC came into service after the most successful period of the war for the submarines, and it was these vessels that were the targets the Allied anti-submarine campaign from 1943 to 1944. This is the vessel that was featured in the film *Das Boot*. It was capable of a speed of 17.7 knots on the surface and 7.6 knots when submerged. It carried fourteen torpedoes and had a surface range of 8,500 miles at an average speed of 10 knots. It carried a crew of between forty-four and fifty-two men, and its deck gun tended to be an 88 mm multi-purpose weapon.

This is *U-7*, a Type IIB that was constructed in Kiel at the Germaniawerft Krupp factory. It was launched on 29 June 1935, and was the first submarine to be manufactured there. The factory would continue operating until the last boat, *U-4710*, was launched on 14 April 1945. Another U-boat, *U-4714*, was under construction and was launched there, but this one was never commissioned. It was launched on 26 April and scuttled on 3 May 1945. *U-7* was primarily used as a school, or front, boat from 1937 until 1944. It sank on 8 February 1944 to the west of Pillau in a diving accident. All twenty-nine crew onboard were killed, including *Oberleutnant zur See* Günther Loeschcke, who had taken over command of the vessel just the previous month. *U-7*, under the command of Werner Heidel, had sunk two vessels in September 1939 – the British steam merchantman *Akenside*, which it stopped with machine-gun fire fifteen miles west by north of Marsten Island on 22 September, and the Norwegian steam merchantman, *Takstaas*, which was carrying lumber, on 29 September. She was stopped by a series of warning shots from the 20 mm gun around ten miles off Marsteinen lighthouse, off Bergen in Norway. The crew abandoned ship, and *U-7* fired a torpedo at her. *Takstaas* began to list and was then fired at by the 20 mm gun. Suddenly Norwegian aircraft arrived and forced *U-7* to submerge. The crew's lifeboats were taken under tow by the Norwegian torpedo-boat *Storm*. The ship itself was taken into tow by a Norwegian tug. The front half of the ship broke away and sank, but the aft was towed in and the cargo salvaged.

A number of Type II submarines in dock. We can clearly see that among them are *U-1*, *U-2* and *U-4*. *U-4* was launched in July 1935 and commissioned the following month. It too had a brief career in action, from September 1939 to April 1940. Under the command of *Kapitän-leutnant* Harro von Klot-Heydenfeldt, *U-4* sank two Finnish vessels on consecutive days, 22 and 23 September 1939, and a Swedish ship on 24 September. The commander was to go on to lead *U-20* on three patrols between January and April 1940, but would lose his life in the Bay of Biscay on 1 July 1940, in command of *U-102*, a Type VIIB. Until relatively recently, the assumption was that this vessel had in fact been lost in the Bay of Biscay, but it now appears that the vessel lies some distance off the south-west coast of Ireland, having been sunk by depth charges from the British destroyer HMS *Vansittart*. All forty-three of *U-102*'s crewmen were killed. *U-4* had one other claim to fame on 10 April 1940, then under the command of *Kapitän-leutnant* Hans-Peter Hinsch. It sank HMS *Thistle* (N24), a T-class British submarine. HMS *Thistle* had fired a spread of four torpedoes at *U-4* to the south-west of Stavanger, Norway. *U-4* evaded them but surfaced at 0213 and fired a spread of two torpedoes. A G7e torpedo hit and sank HMS *Thistle*, and all hands (fifty-three men) were lost. *U-4* was badly damaged at Gotenhafen (now Gdynia, Poland) on 1 August 1944, and was scrapped the following year.

This shows the commander of a Type VII submarine on the conning tower, with other officers and petty officers. Note that they have a collapsible desk for their log and map. The men appear to be in a relaxed mood, so presumably this photograph was taken while the submarine was safely in dock.

A collection of Type II submarines. *U-1*, *U-3* and *U-4* are clearly visible at the front, although it is not possible to identify the other Type IIs in the second rank or the Type II that lies partially concealed in the front row. *U-6*, which is presumably in the photograph, was the vessel commanded by Herbert Brüninghaus, who took this photograph. *U-3* at the outbreak of the war was commanded by *Kapitän-leutnant* Joachim Schepke, who was born in Flensburg in 1912 and died in service on 17 March 1941 in the north Atlantic. His career saw him command *U-3*, *U-19* and *U-100*. He had transferred to the U-boat force in October 1935. It was with *U-3* that he had his first success. On 30 September 1939, at 2108, the Swedish merchantman *Gun* was stopped thirty miles north-west of Hanstholm. A prize crew went on board at 2200 hours. They opened the seacocks and placed charges, but the ship did not sink, and consequently it was sunk on the following day by a single torpedo at 0910. On the same day, 30 September, at 1040, *U-3* stopped the Danish vessel *Vendia* thirty-five miles north-west of Hanstholm. At 1124 the merchantman tried to ram *U-3*. The U-boat fired a badly aimed torpedo, which hit the *Vendia* aft. The stern sank and the rest of the vessel followed after an explosion at 1205. Schepke lost his life at 0318 on 17 March 1941 after being rammed and depth-charged by HMS *Walker* and HMS *Vanoc*. *U-100* had been spotted in heavy fog by early radar, and only six of her crew survived. *U-3* was damaged at Gotenhafen on 1 August 1944, and scrapped the following year.

A close-up of *U-1* coming alongside a German surface vessel. Although *U-1* was the first of these Type IIAs, it was to a large extent the least illustrious of the six commissioned U-boats of its type, primarily because it never really had the opportunity to prove itself in long-term war patrols.

Another close-up, this time of the conning tower of *U-7*. Undoubtedly one of the five men in the conning tower is Adolf Hitler. This seems to be borne out by the sheer numbers of senior officers in full-dress uniform in and around the U-boat. This would presumably have been taken by Brüninghaus, and may well have been the ceremony in which *Kapitän-leutnant* Siegfried Koitschka was awarded the Iron Cross First Class on 7 October 1941. Koitschka was born in August 1917 and only died in May 2002. He had begun his naval career in 1937, transferring to the U-boat service in June 1940. He became commander of the school boat *U-7*. Previous to this he had been the second watch officer on the newly commissioned *U-552*. It was then commanded by *Fregattenkapitän* Erich Topp. Under his command he had sunk a large number of British and Norwegian vessels from March to October 1941. Koitschka himself would go on to command *U-616*, which was located by American destroyers on 14 May 1944 to the east of Cartagena, Spain. Three days later, having been attacked by a destroyer and British Wellingtons, she was forced to surface. The crew scuttled the U-boat and abandoned ship. Koitschka was released from a prisoner-of-war camp in June 1946.

A close-up of the small conning tower of a Type II U-boat. We can clearly see the small hatchway and ladder leading down into the main control compartment of the submarine.

This is a partially submerged *U-38*. *U-38* was launched in August 1938 and commissioned in October. She was primarily a training boat and trial boat. However, she was responsible for sinking thirty-five ships with a total of 188,967 tons. She was a Type IX submarine. *U-38* briefly operated with Prien's wolf pack in June 1940. Owing to her type and age, *U-38* primarily operated at the beginning of the war. Under the command of *Fregattenkapitän* Heinrich Liebe, she sank a number of merchant ships between September 1939 and June 1941. Her most destructive period was March to December 1940, during which time a number of British, Norwegian, Dutch, Belgian, Danish, Greek and Canadian vessels were sunk. In her last period of action, in August 1941, she was commanded by *Fregattenkapitän* Heinrich Schuck, who managed to sink the Panamanian merchantman *Longtaker*. *U-38* was scuttled to the west of Wesermunde on 5 May 1945, and finally broken up in 1948.

Most of the ordinary seamen, probably of a torpedo-boat. The *Torpedoboot 1935* class were an unsuccessful design. They had problems with their high-pressure turbines and they were hard to maintain and repair. They had very little protection against aircraft and were vulnerable. Most of these ships were used for training submarine commanders in the Baltic, which is presumably why Brüninghaus had taken a photograph of this crew. Some of the vessels were put into reserve status as they were too vulnerable to be used during wartime.

Aboard a torpedo-boat. Once again this vessel is being used as a training ship for submarine commanders. Even the replacement *Torpedoboot 1937* class (*T13–T21*) were relegated to U-boat training. Their problem was that they had an imbalanced armament. However, from 1944 some of them were attached to cruisers and German battle groups. Ultimately they were replaced by the *Flottentorpedoboot 1939*, which were more multi-purpose and used for torpedo attacks, escorting and anti-aircraft defence. These tended not to be used for submarine training and were more like a light destroyer.

The two men to the rear of this photograph are wearing *Torpedoboot* insignia on their caps. The men in the front may well be submarine crew under training. Notice that even in this vessel, which is far larger than a submarine, the sleeping arrangements are cramped.

This is a shot of a German surface vessel, which appears to be a *Torpedoboot 1937* class vessel, used for U-boat training purposes. These vessels were in fact commissioned from May 1941 until July 1942. Of the nine built, two were sunk in action. *T-13* was sunk on 10 April 1945, and *T-18* on 17 September 1944. Two (*T-14* and *T-20*) survived the war and were not scrapped until 1951. *T-19* was scrapped in 1952, and the last of its class, *T-17*, was scrapped at some point after 1960.

A posed photograph of German U-boat officers in full-dress uniforms. Note that the officer on the second left has the Iron Cross on his left breast of the jacket. Three of the four men also carry their ceremonial daggers. These men are wearing their small service suits, and all appear to be middling-rank officers; either *Korvettenkapitän*, *Fregattenkapitän* or *Kapitän zur See*.

This is another view on board the torpedo-boat during U-boat commander training. These men are all wearing their *U-Boot Packchen*, which was leather clothing designed to keep out the elements.

This photograph appears to have been taken either just before the outbreak of the war or very early in the war, as it features uniforms that would only have been worn for ceremonial purposes. These men appear to be high-ranking naval officers. All of them are wearing their service suits, which included a jacket, a pair of trousers, white shirt, sash, grey gloves, dagger and peaked cap. As an alternative to this the men could wear their full parade uniform, with their ranks indicated by the number of stripes and the arrangement of epaulettes on the shoulders. In peacetime they would have worn the *Zweispitz* cap, but this was not worn in wartime, indicating that this was probably taken shortly after September 1939.

Unfortunately the cap legend is not visible on this photograph, but the star on the left arm of the man on the left of the picture indicates that he is a naval officer. It is possible that he could be a petty officer, as a yellow version of this star in a blue circular field was worn in this position by both petty officers and men in the German navy. The men who could become officers of the navy were required to be 'intellectually excellent young men with the necessary capabilities and knowledge'.

The German navy preferred those with high academic achievements, but no previous knowledge of the sea was necessary, as this would be taken care of during training.

A posed crew complement. It is not possible to see the words written on the cap badges, but there is certainly a wide variety of senior German naval officers at the front of this group. Many of them carry their decorations on their lower left breast. Some of the men can also be seen to have service badges, and the presumption is that this was taken by Brüninghaus sometime in late 1941 or early 1942. Note that the vessel on which they are all standing is concealed under a camouflage netting arrangement, which extends from the edge of the dockside over the vessel.

Senior German naval officers in full-dress uniform. Officers could choose to become standard naval officers or focus on a particular specialism, such as engineering, technical communications, weapons or torpedoes. All of the branches received the same rate of pay, but those in some areas had to meet certain physical and professional requirements. If an officer or man served for at least twelve years he had an automatic right to a position in the civil service at the end of his naval service. A volunteer could become a petty officer if he signed on for twelve years.

Another shot of the same group of officers, this time saluting. The officer second left has the rank of *Korvettenkapitän*, and is wearing his small service suit with a black cap. The other officers are wearing their regular service suits, which are longer. The officer second left has also been awarded the Iron Cross and has other decorations that are not clearly visible on his left chest area.

This photograph was taken by Brüninghaus, of a dry dock in which three identical torpedo-boats are being readied for service. Of all the German torpedo-boats that were used during the Second World War (fifty-one were built), only twelve actually survived the war. To a large extent the torpedo-boat proved to be almost useless; many were pressed into service for U-boat training, while others were reluctantly used for minelaying, patrols and escort duties. The Germans had believed that torpedo attacks by small boats against larger surface vessels would work just as well as they had done in actions such as the Battle of Jutland in 1916. They proved to be wholly wrong in this assumption. For one thing the torpedo-boats were virtually unable to defend themselves against aerial attack, and the accuracy of enemy shells was far better than it had been just twenty-five years before.

On board a German torpedo-boat, a posed or action shot taken by Brüninghaus. Note that there are a number of crewmen gathered around the gun, purely observing, and that only three or four of the men would normally operate the weapon when it was being used in action. An officer is standing behind the gun and its crew with a range-finding device.

Cleaning out the larger guns on a torpedo-boat. This was the main armament of the vessel besides the torpedoes. By the time the *Flottentorpedoboot (1939)* came into service in early 1942, the Germans had developed one of their best seagoing ships in the *Kriegsmarine*. The bulk of them did not become operational until 1943, and as a result they were mainly used in the Baltic Sea. In all probability this is either a *Torpedoboot 1935* or *1937*, although from the shape of the bridge it could be a *Flottentorpedoboot 1939*. It bears no resemblance to the later versions, the *Flottentorpedoboot 1940, 1941* or *1944*, as these were far larger vessels.

Working with a torpedo off a torpedo-boat. This was vital training for submarine crews. Some torpedoes were powered by a combustion steam engine (alcohol), with three preset speeds, 44 knots, 40 knots or 30 knots. Initially the maximum speed setting was banned, as this overloaded the engine. The other torpedo used was the battery-powered G7E. This featured two counter-rotating, twin-bladed propellers. The battery took up one-third of the mass of the torpedo. As it left no bubbles, it was ideal for making daylight attacks. The G7A, which was the gas steam version, left a telltale trail of bubbles, and tended only to be used for night or long-range attacks. The G7E had been developed in secrecy and in direct contravention of the Treaty of Versailles. It was these torpedoes that were used to sink the British battleship HMS *Royal Oak*. The British had no idea that it had been developed until they recovered parts of the torpedo on the seabed at Scapa Flow.

Here we see artillery shells, laid out ready for firing, beside the main deck gun of a torpedo-boat. Torpedo-boats had been highly successful during the First World War, and notably during the Battle of Jutland. Whole flotillas of these torpedo-boats had been created specifically to attack larger enemy surface vessels. It quickly became clear to the Germans that this was no longer an option open to them, and the torpedo-boat was rapidly relegated to secondary duties. As far as the German navy was concerned, this provided it with a readily available small vessel in which German U-boat commanders could be trained.

This is a German torpedo-boat making its way in a heavy swell. Note that the deck gun beneath the control room has been covered in waterproofing in order to protect it from the worst of the elements.

The German *Kriegsmarine* did not control its own maritime air units during the Second World War. In 1939 the Office of the *General der Luftwaffe beim Oberkommando der Kriegsmarine* was created. Aircraft were used on various *Kriegsmarine* vessels, including *Bismarck* and on some other German cruisers. They were responsible for reconnaissance, patrols, and air support and courier duties. The pilots were trained, controlled and provided by the *Luftwaffe*. The *Kriegsmarine* provided the necessary liaison support. As can be seen in this photograph, the aircraft were mainly float-planes. They were stored above deck, and a catapult was used to launch them into the air. The aircraft would land after its mission in the water alongside the vessel, and a crane would be used to hoist it back onto its launching-place above deck. It was the *Luftwaffe* that also controlled aircraft that took part in attacks on shipping, carried out coastal and sea reconnaissance and patrols, minesweeping operations and air/sea rescue. The Germans used a variety of different aircraft.

German Type 35 and Type 37 torpedo-boats, which, as we have seen, were used for U-boat training. They were originally built in order to get around the Washington Naval Treaty, which had been agreed and signed in 1922. It was designed to limit the naval armaments of the key signatories and impose limits on the defeated nations from the First World War. Germany was also limited in terms of its naval construction by the Treaty of Versailles.

A German torpedo-boat approaching the dock entrance after U-boat training manoeuvres. Between 1934 and the end of the Second World War, upwards of 40,600 officers and men passed through U-boat training. About 500 of the applicants were rejected as being unsuitable. Many of the U-boat commanders had already served on German naval surface vessels. The *Kriegsmarine* created ten torpedo-boat flotillas during the war; the first, for example, operated from the summer of 1940 to the spring of 1941. The last flotilla was created in January 1944, and operated in the Ligurian Sea.

This unidentified major German surface vessel was photographed by Brüninghaus. The German navy called its major warships *Kriegsschiffen*. Within this category there were battleships, armoured ships, battle, heavy and light cruisers, as well as auxiliary cruisers. The smaller destroyers and torpedo-boats were obviously more numerous.

This is another major German surface vessel under way in a photograph taken by Brüninghaus. In all likelihood this photograph was taken just outside Kiel harbour. The Germans had authorised a huge naval building programme in 1937. Work had rapidly begun on two major battleships (*Bismarck* and *Tirpitz*). There were also three pocket battleships under way and two battle cruisers, but when war broke out in 1939 the *Kriegsmarine* was well behind its goal of building a world-class fleet. The sheer speed of the development of the German surface fleet led to deficiencies in the surface vessels. *Admiral Graf Spee*, a pocket battleship, had diesel engines that could not endure more than a thousand hours of continuous operation without a major overhaul. She was also vulnerable in terms of her armour protection. Owing to the lack of numbers and to problems such as these, it would be submarines that would take the brunt of the naval war against the Royal Navy.

The full ship's complement is arrayed on the deck in this photograph, again taken by Brüninghaus. Although Germany had a fairly long sea coast in the north, its only access into the Atlantic was through relatively narrow channels. It quickly became apparent that the English Channel was too well policed by the Royal Navy, and that a similar peril presented itself if surface vessels entered the North Sea and tried to traverse Britain to the north. It quickly became apparent, too, to the Germans that the *Kriegsmarine* was no match for the Royal Navy. The invasion of Norway in 1940, for example, had seen the *Kriegsmarine* losing almost half of its surface vessels. Although the Germans had bases that they needed for their navy, they no longer had the navy to exploit it.

Another photograph of a major German surface vessel, and possibly the same one as shown in the previous photograph, as the crew appears to be parading on deck. The German supreme naval commander, until 1943, was *Grossadmiral* Erich Raeder. He was eventually to be replaced by Karl Dönitz. It was Raeder who suggested the invasions of Denmark and Norway, not only to secure direct exit into the North Sea for his surface vessels and submarines, but also because they would be out of reach of the Royal Air Force. Raeder effectively retired in May 1943, and after the war ended he was sentenced to life at Nuremberg. He was released from prison in September 1955.

This photograph shows the loading of a torpedo into a German submarine. The torpedo was a very sophisticated weapon; the device to detonate the warhead was known as the pistol. There were two types, magnetic and contact. Most of the torpedoes had both types, so the commander could choose a combination or both types before the weapon was launched. The magnetic pistol was triggered by the target vessel's magnetic field. It was designed to explode beneath the hull. This could break the ship in two, but magnetic pistols could detonate prematurely as they approached the wake of the ship. The contact pistols were designed to explode when they hit the target, but a fairly narrow impact angle had to be achieved. A safety device only armed the pistol after 275 yards. As the torpedo moved forward in the water it would spin the propeller until it wound shut and armed the pistol.

In the conning tower of a German U-boat. The Type VII U-boat had a number of different bridge designs. Some of the original bridge designs were modified to take additional anti-aircraft weapons. By the end of the war the Type VII alone had seven different bridge conversions. It was clear to the Germans by the middle of 1942 that Allied air superiority made the single 20 mm flak gun inadequate. The bridge conversions were intended to improve the air defence. The first conversion saw two 20 mm flak guns, although the fourth bridge conversion was considered to be the most effective, as it now allowed two twin 20 mm flak guns side by side, and then to the aft of the bridge a quadruple 20 mm flak gun or a single 37 mm flak gun. All of the guns were fitted with protective shields. The lowered platform to the aft of the bridge was referred to as the *Wintergarten*. The final bridge conversion had a lower area encircling the bridge, with twin 37 mm flak cannon fore and aft. There were other unofficial or customised anti-aircraft configurations.

Another shot of bridge activity on board the German submarine. The Type VII had around forty-five crewmen, a considerable increase over the twenty-five who crewed a Type II. The Type IX had around fifty, and the Type XXI had fifty-seven men on board. The U-boats would often carry specialist crews for particular missions, such as spies, commandos or scientists. Even if the captain was on the bridge he would have one of his watch officers with him, and almost certainly the navigator and a petty officer responsible for communications and sound equipment. The backbone of the German submarine force was of course the Type VII. It was under continuous modification in order to give it a longer range and a better performance, and to improve its armament. It was extremely seaworthy and manoeuvrable, and it was ideal for operating in the north Atlantic. It was also relatively cheap and quick to construct, and did not require a huge crew. These attack boats had a single hull design and had several ballast tanks that were placed both internally and externally of the pressurised hull. Additional saddle-tanks were fitted to the sides of the hull, and the fuel tanks were inside the hull to try to avoid leakages if the submarine came under depth-charge attack.

A German submarine makes its way under the protection of two German surface ships. The various versions of the Type VII varied in surface speed from 16 to 17.2 knots, although the 1942 version of the Type VIIC could reach an optimum 18.6 knots on the surface. The submerged speed was no greater than 8 knots. The boats were designed to operate no deeper than around 650 feet. The length of the vessels also varied as modifications were made. Initially the Type VIIA was 211 ft 7 in. long with a beam of 19 ft and a draft of 14 ft 5 in. The largest version was the Type VIID, which was designed not as an attack boat but as a minelayer. It was 252 ft 3 in. long with a beam of 21 ft and a draft of 16 ft 4 in.

U-38 is shown in this photograph. This vessel was commissioned in October 1938, and throughout its career it would have eight commanders and be engaged in eleven war patrols. In all, *U-38* hit thirty-six enemy or neutral vessels, sinking thirty-five of them (188,967 tons). All of the sinkings were carried out in the early stages of the war. By late 1941 *U-38* had been relegated to a training, trial and school boat. She was only ever attacked on one occasion, by a merchant escort vessel on 2 January 1941. She was depth-charged and suffered minimal damage. *U-38* was attached to Prien's wolf pack in June 1940, during which time she managed to sink three vessels.

Christmas celebrations inside a German U-boat. There was very little privacy on board a submarine. The bunks were either side of the main walkway, and it was impossible to have uninterrupted sleep without other crew members thundering backwards and forwards at all times of the day and night. It was only the commander of the submarine who had any form of privacy, but this was simply a small curtained area. The commander's quarters were right next door to the control room and the radio room, so that he could hear what was going on at any time and be called quickly in an emergency. The crew spent their free time listening to music, playing cards and trying to sleep.

This is one of several photographs that were taken on what is believed to be *U-47*, commanded by *Korvettenkapitän* Günther Prien. Prien was born in 1908, and was one of the most successful U-boat captains of the war. On 14 October 1939 his *U-47* sank HMS *Royal Oak* in Scapa Flow. This was to be the beginning of an illustrious but short career. On his sixth patrol, in June 1940, he sank eight vessels. The German navy wanted Prien to be transferred to a training unit, but he refused. He left Lorient for his tenth patrol on 20 February 1941, and four days later he sank four ships. The last radio message was received from *U-47* on the morning of 7 March. There has been considerable controversy over the fate of *U-47*. For many years the sinking was credited to the British destroyer HMS *Wolverine*, but now it appears that *U-47* was actually hit by one of its own torpedoes, which suffered a failure and circled back on itself.

A particularly clear photograph of a German U-boat commander on what may well be a Type VII. Both the officer and the crewman have the coveted U-boat badge. The design followed an earlier award badge that was used towards the end of the First World War. It depicted a submarine with its bow facing left with a deck gun and a flag aft of the conning tower. It also featured the national emblem of the eagle and swastika. The badge was to be worn on the left breast of all service and dress jackets, jumpers and shirts. In order to be awarded the badge, the individual would have to have been involved in two engagements or sorties, and it could therefore not be awarded to U-boat personnel who were engaged only in shore duties. Originally they were made of gilded brass, but later in the war they were made of zinc with a gilt wash. The badge was instituted by Raeder. The badges are now highly sought after, and some of the earlier adorned examples, with clusters of diamonds, are worth many thousands of pounds.

This is an impressive photograph of a German submarine following a large naval surface vessel through the entrance to a harbour. The presumption is that the U-boat is actually leaving the harbour rather than entering it, as the crewmen are wearing their service suits rather than their parade jackets or walking-out dress. It appears that they are wearing their blue service suits – in other words their standard work wear during operations. Note that the submarine is lashed to the surface vessel, but it is not under tow.

This interesting photograph is taken from the bridge of a German submarine, looking towards a German surface vessel. The sea appears to be partially frozen, so this may imply that the photograph was taken somewhere in the Baltic by Brüninghaus. One of the difficulties in identifying German U-boats is that when the war broke out the numerical markings were discontinued. They had been written about 5 ft high on the conning tower, but now the submarines were all painted in a neutral grey. However, many of the U-boats had their own insignia or emblems. Prien's U-boat, *U-47*, had a snorting bull, and this was adopted as an insignia by the whole 7th U-boat Flotilla. It became practice that when a new commander took over a U-boat he would add his own emblem, and not replace the existing one, as this was deemed to be unlucky. The men would also stitch their emblems onto their own uniforms and caps. Not all of the U-boats had their own insignia, but others could be seen with a variety of different emblems at different times, which causes additional confusion in terms of recognition.

This photograph, taken from a German U-boat, is believed to be of a Junkers Ju 88. It was originally designed as a fast bomber, but it was used extensively to support U-boats. It was also extensively used from 1942 in the Bay of Biscay on anti-shipping patrols and escort missions. Routinely they encountered British aircraft, notably Beaufighters, and later in the war, Mosquitoes. As the Allied aircraft became more numerous, Focke-Wulf Fw 190 fighters with long-range fuel tanks were also deployed. The key battles in the skies over the Bay of Biscay took place in the summer of 1943, with Germany decidedly losing the air war. The aircraft from *KG40*, the *Luftwaffe* formation responsible for the region, suffered catastrophic casualties during and immediately after the Allied landings in Normandy in June 1944. The losses were so great that by the following month the unit was disbanded.

A German submarine engages an incoming, attacking Allied aircraft with its flak gun. In all probability this is a British Beaufighter, in effect a long-range version of the Beaufort. It was extensively used by Coastal Command during the war. The aircraft was also used in an anti-shipping role, and at least 117 enemy vessels were sunk by these aircraft. The Beaufighter had four forward-firing 20 mm cannon fitted to the lower fuselage. It also had six 7.7 mm Browning machine-guns. The aircraft saw enormous numbers of modifications throughout the war, although usually if a Beaufighter had a C in its description this meant that it had been converted for use by Coastal Command. It had an impressive range of just over 1,740 miles, and it could also be fitted with torpedoes and rockets. The Coastal Command version also often had a Vickers gas-operated rapid-firing machine-gun or a .303 Browning. It could achieve a maximum speed of 320 mph.

On board a German U-boat two crew members clean and test the anti-aircraft gun, while the watch officer and another crew member look on. The ever-present fear of being caught on the surface by enemy aircraft meant that the anti-aircraft weapons had to be kept in tip-top condition. The weapon being worked on here is a 20 mm flak cannon. When the submarines were fitted with a naval version of the army's 37 mm flak gun in late 1943, it gave them slightly more chance of fending off an attack. However, the 37 mm gun proved to be extremely sensitive to the seawater, and it had to be serviced on a far too regular basis. A submarine was not expected to stay above the surface and fight it out with enemy aircraft, as it was simply unlikely to win. The best defence for the submarines was to be on constant alert, and if an enemy aircraft were spotted, to dive without hesitation.

A German U-boat makes good progress on the surface and flies its naval flag from the rear of the conning tower. By the middle of 1942, with radar making surfaced U-boats easy to pinpoint, a warning device was developed that would inform the U-boat crew if it had been illuminated on Allied radar. Some of the early versions were disastrous, and the Allies were able to home in on signals that were emitted by the warning device itself. When the Metox was introduced in August 1942, U-boat crews found that they became a beacon for Allied aircraft. The Wanze, which came in a year later, was almost completely ineffective. The Borkum was brought in as a stop-gap measure. This gave an audible warning, and although it had limited functionality it was better. Other versions were brought in during the later part of the war, such as the Naxos, Tunis, Bali and the Athos.

This is a close-up photograph of the delicate process of loading a torpedo beneath the deck of a submarine. Note that the trolley holding the torpedo has small wheels that are designed to roll along the slats of the deck's surface. This would enable the crews to line up the torpedo so that it could be more easily fitted into the hatch. The G7A and G7E were the most common types of torpedo, but at the end of 1942 a new anti-convoy weapon was introduced. It was programmed to run in a straight line for a specified distance, and if it had not hit a target it would change course by turning either left or right, and run for another period before changing course again. In effect the torpedo had the ability to zigzag across the path of a convoy, improving the chances of scoring a hit. Another type of torpedo was also used as an anti-escort weapon. This torpedo had a combination of magnetic and contact pistols. It could travel at 24.5 knots and had a range of 6,300 yards. It was not enormously effective, and it was not unknown for the torpedo to simply turn around and sink the U-boat. In order to avoid this unfortunate incident, U-boats would fire the torpedo and then dive as deeply as they possibly could, as quickly as was practicable. This type of torpedo was an acoustic homing version, but the Allies had already begun to introduce Foxer, effectively a noise maker that was towed behind warships to decoy the acoustic sensors.

The snorkel of a German U-boat pokes ominously above the surface in this photograph. The snorkel was absolutely essential as the Germans began to lose the battle of the Atlantic. The U-boats ran on their electric engines when they were under water because the diesel engines needed air and were therefore useless. This meant that the U-boats had a limited range and speed. They would need to surface and run the diesel engines in order to recharge the electric batteries. The snorkel changed all of this; it allowed the U-boats to use their diesel engines underwater. The snorkel was, in essence, a pipe with a valve at one end. There was an intake and an exhaust pipe, which allowed air to be drawn into the U-boat and the engines' exhaust gases to be expelled. A valve prevented seawater from getting down the pipes if the tube went below the surface of the water. This gave the U-boats an enormous tactical advantage. However, they were not foolproof, and waves could sweep over the head of the snorkel and water would be drawn in. The other problem, of course, was that running the diesel engines underwater meant that the U-boat could be more easily heard. The snorkel originally also caused problems with the periscope, as the wake and the fumes affected the vision. Ultimately the snorkel head was put at the rear of the boat, but even this did not save the U-boats from being detected. Allied radar could pick up a snorkel head at a range of around three miles. The Germans responded by covering the snorkel heads with a substance known as *Tarnmatte*, which supposedly was radar absorbing.

Bibliography

Buchheim, Lothar-Gunther, *U-boat War*, Alfred A. Knopf, 1978

Compton-Hall, Richard, *Submarines at War 1914–1918*, Macmillan, 1991

Macintyre, Donald, *The Battle of the Atlantic*, Pen & Sword, 2006

Mars, Alastair, *Unbroken*, Pen & Sword, 2008

Vause, Jordan, *U-boat Ace*, Naval Institute Press, 2003

Werner, Herbert, *Iron Coffins*, Cassell, 1999

Williams, Andrew, *The Battle of the Atlantic*, BBC Books, 2003

Williamson, Gordon, *Wolfpack,* Osprey, 2006

Useful websites:
  www.uboat.net
  www.uboataces.com
  www.kriegsmarine-reich.co.uk
  www.feldgrau.com
  www.ubootwaffe.net